The guidance given in this book relates solely to general astrological considerations. For detailed advice regarding your personal situation, consult a qualified professional practitioner in the relevant field.

YOUR HOROSCOPE 2021

LIBRA

ZOE BUCKDEN

LIBRA

GENERAL TRENDS

This year is all about the battle between duty and freedom. Rebellious Uranus is currently travelling through stubborn Taurus and locked in conflict with stern Saturn in revolutionary Aquarius. This sets the drive for freedom against the demands of duty, individual desire against family commitments and social obligations.

There are many ways in which this tension can play out. New technologies versus established institutions, youth against age, rebellion against oppression. Progress may be held back by ossified structures, hot-headed vandalism destroy age-old wisdom, truth be beaten down by power, and patience thrown aside by impulse. This is a fierce astrological landscape, marvellous in retrospect but difficult to live through.

The conflict will be sharpened by many factors. Uranus is the ruler of Aquarius, so the influence of Saturn in this sign will have a strong dampening effect. Think of a newly-minted adult just starting to carve their own path in the world, but being called home by the needs of elderly relatives or long-standing family obligations. Saturn has just left Capricorn, and is strengthened by its three-year journey through its own home sign – and since Taurus is an earth sign like Capricorn, the planet's voice will be heard clearly there. Finally, mighty Jupiter is travelling alongside Saturn and will lend its expansive, positive influence to this cold and cautious planet.

In other words, the repressive effects of sensible Saturn will be stronger than usual, enough to hamper even rebellious Uranus' bid for freedom. That won't stop progress from happening in the long run, but it will cause enormous tension to build before the inevitable crash occurs.

The upside is that caution has its uses, and even an old dog can sometimes learn new tricks. Saturn is not an enemy of progress. It merely reminds us that many things have been tried before with terrible results, and that we'd be wise to look before we leap. Likewise, with Uranus in a sympathetic sign, it may be possible to embrace the advantages of change without breaking important links with the past.

Since both planets are slow-moving, the tension between them won't resolve in a hurry. We're also more likely to feel these forces through global and societal events, rather than in matters close to home. But the overall tension between duty and freedom will inform all our experiences this year, and provide a lens through which we can can view the events of our own individual lives more clearly.

For you personally, the conflict will be strongest in the areas of home, family, love (including romance and children, but also creative projects and anything you're passionate about), shared property, and inheritance (including childhood issues and emotional "baggage" of all kinds). Your everyday routines (including your neighbourhood and workplace) may be affected as well, since this house is ruled by Jupiter.

There will be a lot to unpack. Think of this time as a cosmic clearout of your home environment. Despite the dust and mess and upheaval, you'll eventually emerge into a space that's fresh and clean and suitable for what you want to do. Hold on to that vision, and everything that follows will be a mere temporary inconvenience.

The tension won't last forever. By spring next year, you'll begin to see the shape of a resolution. In the meantime, take a good long look at these areas of your life. Are they all that you want them to be?

You may feel trapped, frustrated, and held back by rigid constraints. Do remember that in every challenge there is also an opportunity. The upsets, obstacles, and confrontations that occur may be telling you something. Perhaps it's time for a change.

Stay open to possibilities, and you'll reap rich rewards.

On a positive note, powerful Pluto in beautiful angle to idealistic Neptune lends strength and dignity to the argument. This could transform your understanding of duty and obligation. If you choose to make drastic changes in your life, make sure you understand the consequences. Conversely, if circumstances force you to seek new pastures, look for the tender shoots of growth.

It's a wonderful time to get in touch with your own innermost self, and act in accordance with your highest ideals. Whatever passes from your life during these years is clearing the way for a better future. By living true to yourself, you'll manifest more fully your own chosen destiny.

The Gemini-Sagittarius eclipse series that began in 2020 continues in May and June, bringing significant changes to your houses of travel, learning, and everyday routines during the early summer months. The series ends with a solar eclipse in Sagittarius in early December, signalling a fresh start in your house of everyday routines (including your neighbourhood and workplace). This final eclipse marks the end of the transformation the series has brought to your life. There will be no more eclipses on the Gemini-Sagittarius axis until 2029.

Idealistic Neptune in dreamy Pisces will be involved in these eclipses, which could bring a fog of confusion and the risk of wishful thinking. Don't plan to start anything important during this time of uncertainty. It's fine to respond to events if you must, but make sure you have all the facts.

Since Pisces is your house of health and work (which includes all the practical steps you take in pursuit of your goals), you may be especially prone to mistakes or confusion. Make sure you know what you're doing. Seek professional advice if required.

A new eclipse series starts on the Taurus-Scorpio axis towards the end of the year, opening with a lunar eclipse in Taurus in mid-November. This will add to the upheaval in your house of shared property and inheritance, so expect the unexpected! Jupiter and Saturn add their input from your house of love. Matters connected with home, family, and everyday routines may be involved as well.

The series will transform the areas of money and property for you, concluding with a lunar eclipse in Taurus during late October 2023. The balance between what's truly your own and what belongs to others will shift. Whatever comes to light this year may not be fully resolved until the series has finished, so be patient and let the universe speak. You have plenty of time!

Also towards the end of the year, your ruling planet Venus turns retrograde in Capricorn, your house of home and family. With plenty of other planets rallying around in support, this isn't likely to be troublesome. It's a time to slow down and enjoy domestic life. Plan for a pleasant Christmas (or other holiday) among those you care about the most.

Your birthday month this year will be dominated by Mercury retrograde in your own sun sign of Libra, followed by a beautiful new moon in early October.

This is a time to review and reflect, clear out the old and make a start on the new. Consider what you truly want in life. Mercury rules your houses of inner needs, travel, and learning, so this is an excellent opportunity to set the right course for the future.

The most stable areas of your life this year will be relationships, friendships, and your social life in general. No major changes are due, so enjoy things as they are.

January

The year opens with a party in Capricorn, your house of home and family. The mighty Sun, powerful Pluto, and clear-thinking Mercury are all sharing out champagne and making bold plans for the year ahead. Expansive Jupiter and sensible Saturn (the ruler of Capricorn), both in Aquarius, add their toasts from your house of love. This is going to be a great new year!

Except that... There's always a 'but' in the cold light of dawn. Belligerent Mars in fiery Aries throws down the gauntlet of challenge in your relationship house, and erratic Uranus retrograde in stubborn Taurus (your house of shared property and inheritance) adds its own frustrated energy to the mix. Maybe those brilliant late-night plans weren't so fabulous after all. But then, maybe staying put and trying to make things work is just another way of giving up on freedom.

These are complex energies, and the answers to the questions they pose may be complex as well. With so many slow-moving planets involved, the situation won't resolve in a hurry. But there's definitely hope! The Sun and Uranus are in lovely angle to each other, which promises an excellent conclusion. It may just take a bit of time.

On Wednesday 6 Mars moves into your house of shared property and inheritance, and connects with Uranus retrograde in that house. This sharpens the conflict with Saturn in your house of love. The tension will dominate the next few weeks, so expect plenty of headaches before Mars moves out of range at the end of the month.

You may experience problems within important relationships, especially connected with close family or other loved ones. Money quarrels or disputes over property may come to the fore.

On Friday 8 Venus, the ruler of Taurus, moves into fellow earth sign Capricorn, your house of home and family. This will soothe inflamed feelings and help everyone move towards agreement.

Constructive talks may begin at once, but if you can delay matters for a week or so, the new moon in Capricorn at midmonth will set the stage for a new phase in discussions. Hold off on engaging until then if you can.

Chatty Mercury moves into Aquarius on the same day, so expect news or other developments in the realm of love. With Pluto and Saturn in close attendance, weighty matters may come to the fore. Listen carefully, but don't make decisions in haste. You have plenty of time to consider whatever comes to light. For now, let the universe speak.

On Wednesday 13 January, a new moon in Capricorn offers the chance for a fresh start in your domestic life. This is a lovely new moon, with powerful Pluto in close support and idealistic Neptune sending blessings from your house of health and work. Use this beautiful energy for a positive new take on matters close to home.

The very next day, Thursday 14, Uranus turns direct in your house of shared property and inheritance. Suddenly those strong blocks and heavy obligations don't seem so formidable any more! It will take a while for everything to start moving forward, but you may well feel as if a weight has been lifted from your shoulders. Pay attention to any strange or unusual events in the days surrounding this date.

A few days afterwards, on Tuesday 19, the Sun moves into Aquarius and shifts the planetary focus to your house of love. Uranus, the ruler of this house, and aggressive Mars are both in hard angle, which suggests fierce conflicts and chaotic disarray. This may affect your loved ones rather than yourself, so stand by to offer support as needed.

Be mindful of safety. Avoid risk. Keep a very close eye on any children in your life.

If you're keen to get projects off the ground, especially anything close to your heart, a new moon in Aquarius in mid-February offers a better opportunity. Hold off until then if you can. If you can afford to wait a few months, a new moon in Virgo in early September provides an excellent alternative. Make your preparations now!

Towards the end of the month, on Thursday 28 January, a full moon in Leo brings something to an end in your house of friendship. This is a difficult full moon, with hard angles to combative Mars and revolutionary Uranus in your house of shared property and inheritance. Existing problems within your social circle could reach a crisis point. You may despair of ever finding a way forward.

Your instincts are exactly right! Whatever ends now has probably had its day. Let it go. Wonderful new things are in the offing, but while you remain tangled up in this particular issue you may not even notice them.

Powerful Pluto and inspirational Neptune are deep in conversation, bringing profound insight to your houses of home, family, health, and work. This could open a new era in your life! Release the past, and look forward to a wonderful future. The planets will guide you.

Letting go may prove more difficult than it sounds. On Saturday 30, communicative Mercury turns retrograde in your house of love. Past issues may crowd your thinking. Spats and misunderstandings with loved ones are likely.

Don't do anything in haste. You have many weeks to process this information. Nothing needs to be settled until late February at the earliest, and full resolution may not happen until the summer months. By all means deal with matters as they arise, but don't feel obliged to finish anything once and for all. There's plenty of time to consider your options.

February

The month opens with a fillip of power in your house of home and family. Harmony planet Venus in close conversation with powerful Pluto brings gentle strength to domestic life. If you've struggled to make meaningful changes close to home, the first week of this month offers a fantastic opportunity. Make your move now!

On Thursday 11 February, a new moon in Aquarius signals a fresh beginning in your house of love. With a cluster of planets gathered in this house, there's a strong push for change. The problem is that Mars and Uranus in your house of shared property and inheritance simply aren't interested. With these two energy planets blocking your path, there won't be any significant progress.

Don't let that bring you down! Change will happen eventually – just not yet.

If you have projects to get off the ground, launch them a few days later if you can. After mid-month, the obstacles will clear and you'll begin to see the road ahead.

Mercury is still retrograde, which brings snags and snarlups to everyone's life. It's not a great time to do anything important. Just hang fire for a while.

On Thursday 18 the Sun moves into Pisces, bringing

fresh emphasis to your house of health and work. Two days later, on Saturday 20, communication planet Mercury turns direct. The combined effect will involve major confusion. Play things safe, and don't enter into agreements of any kind until you've clarified every clause and nailed down every detail.

On Thursday 25, harmony planet Venus moves into water sign Pisces, your house of health and work. This brings a lovely merging of sympathetic energies, so expect a blissful few weeks. It may seem as if a spell of harmony and joy has fallen upon the world, and for once everyone shows themselves at their best.

You'll notice this new tranquillity more strongly than most, since Venus rules your own sun sign of Libra. Towards the end of the month and throughout early March, you may feel you can do no wrong. Bliss and serenity reign supreme. Why can't life always be like this?

People and the world being what they are, this strange and wonderful truce won't last. But do enjoy it while you can!

It's not a great time to start anything new. With a full moon approaching, this is a time of fulfilment and conclusion. Just let matters settle into their natural rhythm.

Saturday 27 brings a full moon in Virgo, your house of inner needs. With a cluster of benevolent planets gathered together in dreamy Pisces, opposite, and adventurous Uranus in helpful angle, this could bring a happy ending to something of personal importance.

Your house of love is another story, as a cluster of planets pick a fight with Uranus in your house of shared property and inheritance (which also covers childhood issues and emotional "baggage" of all kinds). Something will come to an end at this time, and the news won't be good. But you're already seeing the upside, and may even feel a sense of relief. Lay the past to rest, and move forward into a bold new future. The stars are cheering you on!

March

The first week of the month may seem like a haze of bliss. The mighty Sun, idealistic Neptune, and harmonious Venus are all clustered together in dreamy Pisces, building castles in the sky. Adventurous Uranus in happy angle in sensible Taurus tells you to go for it! Surely this time, the stars really have aligned. What could possibly go wrong?

Well, one or two things. Sensible Saturn and clear-sighted Mercury, aided by expansive Jupiter, are raising points of order from your house of love.

Take a moment to consider any objections raised. Gather information before you commit.

If you've prepared the ground, and you're honestly sure your bold new idea is worth investing in (whether this means time, money, or energy), launch it in the days following the new moon in Pisces at mid-month. For an extra boost, press the start button on or after Tuesday 16, as Mercury will be in full direct motion and bringing its shrewd insight to everything you do.

This mid-month new moon on Saturday 13 is a glorious one, full of hopeful energy. The Sun, Moon, Neptune, and Venus all cluster together in your house of health and work, while powerful Pluto sends blessings from your house of home and family. Whatever it is you want to do, the stars are with you!

If you can wait a few days longer, you'll get a fabulous extra boost. On Saturday 20 the Sun moves into fiery Aries, and the zodiac year begins. This creates a boost of fresh new energy that turbo-charges all your schemes. Anything connected with other people and important relationships (whether personal or professional) is especially blessed, but you'll feel the effects in every area of your life. Enjoy!

Do act now, though, and don't delay. Towards the end of the month, a full moon in your own sun sign of Libra brings a time of completion and fulfilment. With plenty of support among the other planets, you'll find that things are coming to a natural conclusion. This is an excellent moment to finish up projects that truly matter in your life.

If you're not quite ready yet, look for ways to conclude whatever you're working on right now. Beautiful full moons during summer and autumn will set the stage for a grand finale. Until then, just sign off on whatever you feel has been done and done right.

April

The first week of the month is full of harmonious energy. All over the zodiac wheel, planets are reaching out to each other in friendly greeting. Everything connected with the people and places that matter in your life is particularly blessed. It seems you can't put a foot wrong!

The new moon in Aries on Monday 12 brings a fresh start in your house of relationships (whether personal or professional). It's a great time to launch joint projects or extend a friendly hand. Aries is the 'birth sign' of the zodiac, so new beginnings and anything connected with youth and renewal is wonderfully blessed right now. Reach for the stars!

In the week that follows, several planets move from Aries into Taurus, sign of fertility and growth. What Aries begins, Taurus continues, so you may already see the effects of things started under the new moon. There's plenty more to come, as matters won't reach their conclusion for another six months or so. Expect a conclusion of some kind during late autumn.

If you're planning a summer holiday, book now if you can. Mercury retrograde and the Gemini-Sagittarius eclipses will bring confusion during the next few months. Buy insurance too, if you feel you might need it. The outlook for summer is unsettled.

On Monday 19 the Sun moves into Taurus, energising your house of shared property and inheritance. With Venus, ruler of Taurus, and communicative Mercury both in attendance, you're likely to hear significant news. Happy beams from Jupiter and Mars suggest the news is to your benefit, but hard angles to Pluto and Saturn indicate major obstacles. You may run into powerful opposition.

Listen carefully, and don't dismiss objections out of hand. There is a solution, and it may be even better than your original idea. Take note of whatever comes up, but don't be deterred. The planets are with you!

Whatever your plans might be, now is not the time to push them through. The new moon in Taurus next month provides a fabulous opportunity for action. In the meantime, just get your ducks in a row.

You may begin to see new possibilities towards the end of the month, as energy planet Mars moves into your house of career. Normally this wouldn't be an ideal placement, as fiery Mars isn't at its best in sensitive water sign Cancer, but helpful beams from other planets could bring remarkable synergy to this unlikely pairing. You may experience fresh energy and renewed determination.

On Tuesday 27 a full moon in Scorpio brings something to an end in your house of money and personal property. This is a difficult full moon, with erratic Uranus close to the Sun in your house of shared property and inheritance, opposite, and stern Saturn (ruler of your house of home and family) in hard angle in your house of love. Insurmountable obstacles or family opposition may put an end to a matter close to your heart.

Don't despair! Pluto, ruler of Scorpio, turns retrograde at around the same time. This weakens forward momentum, and may leave you feeling powerless. But the answers lie in the past, and by using this backward-looking energy you may yet find a way to prevail.

Be patient. Consider the lessons you have learned so far, and use them to strengthen your plans. When Pluto turns direct in late autumn, you'll have a chance to implement them – and a November new moon in Scorpio gives you the perfect opportunity to do so. Bide your time until then.

May

This month the planetary focus shifts to Gemini, your house of travel and learning (the "travel" of the mind).

Major changes are afoot. Both the mighty Sun and communicative Mercury, the ruler of Gemini (as well as your house of inner needs), will spend several weeks expanding your mental and physical horizons. In addition, a solar eclipse next month opens a whole new chapter in your life.

Keep your plans flexible. You don't yet know how things are likely to shake out.

Do spend a little time thinking about your aims, hopes, and dreams. The new moon in Taurus at mid-month provides an excellent opportunity to consider (or reconsider) your long-term goals. It's a good time to learn from experience, as the backward-looking energy of Mercury's impending retrograde brings up issues from the past.

Don't make any firm commitments regarding the future. Just allow yourself to revisit existing reality. This will provide greater clarity about your true aim in life.

You may begin to feel the effects of all this planetary activity right from the start of the month. Pay attention to any messages that arrive at this time, as they may give you a clue to what's coming next.

The first week of the month is also an excellent time to review your situation in the realm of shared property and inheritance (which includes material resources such as loans and investments, but also spiritual resources such as your family background and heritage, childhood issues, and emotional "baggage" of all kinds). Brush off your plans, especially any that were stymied last month. Your personal ruling planet Venus brings harmonious energy to all that you do. The new moon in Taurus on Tuesday 11 provides an opportunity for launch.

Do make sure you're acting on well-laid plans, and that you've carefully considered any objections raised. Saturn in hard angle will show up any flaws, and Pluto retrograde encourages you to look backwards rather than forwards. Don't let ambition overtake practicality.

(As always, seek professional advice before making any significant decisions regarding money or property.)

At mid-month, a major shift occurs in the areas of love, health, and work. For the past year, protective Jupiter has brought its expansive energy to your house of love (which includes romance and children, but also creative projects and anything you're passionate about).

On Thursday 13 Jupiter leaves this house and moves into Pisces, your house of health and work (meaning the practical steps you take to turn your dreams into reality). With Mars in fellow water sign Cancer, your house of career, you may experience heightened emotion or intense determination regarding your goals.

It's an excellent time to act, provided you've thought things through. If you're sure of what you want, go for it!

Jupiter will remain in Pisces for the next few months before retrograding back into Aquarius at the end of July. Anything that hasn't quite happened for you, especially regarding matters close to your heart, will get a second chance then.

Likewise, issues you thought were done with may crop up again in late summer and early autumn. Jupiter won't move on for good until the end of the year, so you'll have plenty of time to put things to bed. In the meantime, enjoy the benefits of this planet's wonderful energy.

From mid-month onwards, planetary energy shifts decisively towards Gemini, your house of travel and learning. Mercury and Venus are already passing through this sign, and the mighty Sun joins them on Thursday 20.

With a full moon and lunar eclipse looming in Sagittarius, opposite, this is not the time to make big decisions or push through your own demands. Keep a low profile. Listen more than you speak. Major changes are coming, so stay alert and prepare to be flexible.

On Sunday 23 Saturn turns retrograde in Aquarius while in hard angle to Uranus, the ruler of this sign, in stubborn Taurus. This makes for an explosive situation. Keep your head down if you can.

Deep frustration and significant problems are likely, especially concerning your loved ones or anything close to your heart. Be patient! Don't try to push anything through. Just let the universe speak. The issues may resolve themselves, given time.

Be mindful of safety. Uranus energy is erratic. Accidents or other mishaps are possible. Keep a close eye on any children in your life. Avoid risk.

On Wednesday 26 a full moon and lunar eclipse in Sagittarius ends a chapter in your house of everyday routines (including your neighbourhood and workplace). This continues the Gemini-Sagittarius eclipse series that started in early June last year. Then, something came to an end in your everyday life. Now you face another ending, and perhaps a more conclusive one.

The current eclipse is a straight shoot-out between the Moon in Sagittarius and the Sun in Gemini. Jupiter in hard angle in Pisces may bring unwelcome revelations. Hold off on taking important actions until the road ahead becomes clear.

There's a lot of fog and confusion around, so strive for clarity. Saturn retrograde in Aquarius is in helpful angle and may bring knowledge or wisdom from the past. Be guided by experience. An older person or mentor figure may offer sound advice.

Listen to your loved ones, especially close family or anyone within your own trusted domestic circle.

The series concludes in December this year with a solar new moon eclipse in Sagittarius. You may find that the true message of the series doesn't reveal itself until then, or even later. Hold fire if you can. Don't make any long-term commitments. The world may look very different in 2022.

Right at the end of the month, on Saturday 29, Mercury turns retrograde in your travel house, which it rules. With supportive Venus, your personal ruler, close by, and protective Jupiter in friendly angle, this isn't likely to be troublesome, but it's yet another reason to do as little as possible.

Neptune in hard angle suggests confusion and misunderstanding, so be wary of anything you hear. Strive for clarity in all your dealings.

Expect snags and snarlups in the areas of equipment, communication, and travel. Avoid signing contracts or making agreements of any kind (if you can). If you absolutely must deal with anything official, triple check every detail.

Mercury will continue retrograde until late June, and the effects will last into July, so expect confusion to reign during the next few weeks. Do as little as possible.

June

During the first week of this month, you may be in a strange mood. Although things look bright enough on the outside, especially in the professional arena, you may feel apprehensive or strangely ill at ease. If so, this is most likely due to a cross-current of conflict along the Cancer-Capricorn axis, which affects your houses of home, family, and career.

The root of the problem is a showdown between fiery Mars in emotional Cancer, your career house, and powerful Pluto in no-nonsense Capricorn, your house of home and family. But there are complicating factors. Pluto is retrograde, which weakens its power. It also makes the past loom large. With Saturn and Mercury likewise in retrograde motion, there is a natural tendency to look backwards rather than forwards. Hard angles between planets in changeable Gemini and dreamy Pisces add uncertainty, doubt, and confusion to an already frazzled mix.

What is right, and what is wrong? As June opens, you may not be entirely sure of the answer. The good news is that hesitation is not only natural, but healthy. We must question ourselves at times, or else grow rigid and narrow-minded.

Embrace the uncertainty! Idealistic Neptune in happy angle to duelling planets will show the way towards an ethical solution. Compromise and understanding are possible. Just let things flow towards their own conclusion.

There's another reason to sit back and let things happen, rather than risk meddling too much. On Thursday 10 a new moon solar eclipse in Gemini opens a new chapter in your house of travel and learning (the "travel" of the mind). This continues the Gemini-Sagittarius eclipse series that began in early June last year. The series will finish in December this year, having overhauled your houses of travel, learning, and everyday routines (including your neighbourhood and work-place).

The current eclipse is the final one in Gemini, so whatever begins now will last until the next series, which opens in 2029. That's cause for celebration, because this is a positive and helpful eclipse. The Sun and the Moon close to-gether in Gemini receive clarity from retrograde Mercury nearby, while sensible Saturn retrograde in Aquarius adds weight to knowledge and experience.

News and information may arrive regarding matters from the past. Take such communications seriously. They may con-tain the answer to a present-day conundrum.

Clarity of thought and sound reasoning are at a premium right now. Idealistic Neptune in hard angle in dreamy Pisces suggests confusion and wishful thinking, perhaps even out-right deception. Keep your wits about you!

Don't sign contracts or make any firm agreements if you

can possibly avoid it. If you must act, make sure you know what you're doing. Seek professional advice if required.

Above all, stay grounded. Don't do anything in haste. The world will still be there when the fog clears. Wait and see.

This may be harder than it sounds. The very next day, Friday 11, energy planet Mars moves into congenial fire sign Leo, your house of friendship and belonging. With idealistic Neptune in helpful angle, you may feel as if you know exactly what to do. The trouble is, circumstances are changing rapidly. Your chosen path may not look as tempting a few weeks or months from now.

Retrograde Pluto in your house of home and family, opposite, suggests you may feel dragged down or held back by domestic issues. Consider the possibility that this is not an obstacle, but a timely reminder of what genuinely matters to you. Pay attention to reasonable concerns, and stay true to your values. Whatever is right for you will still be right in a month or so. There's no reason to rush into things.

On Monday 21 the Sun moves into Cancer, energising your house of career and public image (including how other people see you). This coincides with hard angles all over the zodiac wheel, so you may feel as if all the troubles of the world have come upon you.

Take heart! Most of the issues arise from combative Mars in fiery Leo, picking fights with powerful Pluto, stern Saturn, and erratic Uranus – all strong-minded, slow-moving planets who won't take any nonsense from fierce but callow youths.

Intense conflict and ferocious disagreements are likely in most areas of your life. Don't take it personally! Even the planets need to clear the air at times, and we mortals are wise to leave them to it. Tread softly, and wait for peace to be restored.

Also at this time, in the days surrounding Sunday 20, money and health matters may come to the fore. Jupiter in Pisces turns retrograde, while making happy connections with the Sun and Moon.

This is an excellent time to focus on your own personal goals in life. Take a break from all the drama!

On Tuesday 22 Mercury turns direct in your travel house, after having been retrograde since late May. You'll feel the static in the air, so move with caution and don't believe everything you hear. Strive for clarity in all your dealings.

Avoid travel if you can. If you must go, allow generous margins and triple check every detail.

Likewise, if you're taking courses or sitting examinations at this time, make absolutely certain you've got everything straight. Saturn retrograde in lovely angle will help you stay focused. Good luck!

It's a good time to finish things up, especially close to home, as a full moon in Capricorn on Thursday 24 brings domestic matters to a conclusion. With retrograde Jupiter in helpful angle, it's an excellent time to review the past.

Anything connected with work or health is also ripe for a happy ending.

Right at the end of the month, matters connected with love and friendship may take an ugly turn, as the emotional Moon passes over retrograde Saturn locked in conflict with fiery Mars. Erratic Uranus throws elements of the unexpected into the mix, which won't help at all.

Keep a close eye on your loved ones, especially any children in your life. Be mindful of safety. Avoid risk.

That said, any upsets are more likely to concern money or property matters. Stay calm, and keep a clear head. The situation will take a long time to resolve in full, so there's no need to leap into action. Bide your time.

July

This month the planetary focus is on Cancer, your house of career. The mighty Sun is in this sign as the month opens, deep in conversation with rebellious Uranus and protective Jupiter.

Change is coming, although its footsteps may be quiet at first. Look to the past for inspiration and enlightenment.

Do think about what you really want from your professional life. If you already have plans, dust them off and make sure they're ready. The new moon in Cancer on Saturday 10 provides an excellent opportunity to set things in motion.

If you're not quite prepared yet, a wonderful new moon in Capricorn on 2 January 2022 provides a fantastic alternative. Delay until then if you feel it's right to do so, as you'll have fabulous planetary support. Obstacles that now seem insurmountable may simply melt away.

Whatever your plans are, events under this new moon may prompt you to take a fresh look at the areas of home, family, and career. The recent eclipse series on the Cancer-Capricorn axis, which ended a year ago, shook things up thoroughly. You may only just be settling into the new normal.

Give yourself a chance to acclimatise before making any momentous decisions. There's plenty of time.

On Thursday 22 the Sun moves into congenial fire sign Leo, bringing light and warmth to the summer months.

This doesn't meet with universal approval, though. Pluto retrograde in Capricorn, and Saturn (the ruler of Capricorn) retrograde in Aquarius, unite in opposition.

With the emotional Moon joining them, the stage is set for conflict.

The full moon in Aquarius on Saturday 24 brings matters to a head. You may experience an unyielding standoff between your house of friendship on one hand, and your houses of love, home, and family on the other. Either your desires are thwarted by obstacles and opposition, or else you may find yourself sidelined by people who ride roughshod over your wishes and beliefs.

This is a difficult climate, but don't despair. Neptune retrograde in your house of health and work invites you to stick to your principles and deal charitably with others. Take the high road! Compromise may be possible, if you extend a friendly hand. Whatever happens under this full moon, don't let it rattle you. Allow things to come to a natural conclusion. The future is bright!

You may hear encouraging news within days of the full moon, as chatty Mercury moves into Leo and protective Jupiter retrogrades into Aquarius, opposite. During the next few weeks, these two planets will meet to discuss fresh possibilities.

Talks may be heated at first. If late July and early August bring sudden upsets, put it down to planetary forces. Things will resolve themselves in time.

Other than that, the last few days of the month are likely to bring a happy bustle of activity. It's an excellent time to finish things up. Get out that to-do list and start ticking things off! Energetic Mars moves into tidy-minded Virgo on Friday 30, providing lots of energy for all those little things that never quite get done. Jupiter retrograde in Aquarius, opposite, will remind you of any backlog.

Approach tasks in a positive spirit. If you can, set the weekend aside for dealing with "stuff". Then roll your sleeves up, and dig in. You'll be glad you did!

August

After the upheaval of the past few months, you may be ready for a summer break. Don't relax just yet! The Sun and Mercury close together in fiery Leo make hard angles with erratic Uranus and stern Saturn, whose long dispute overshadows much of this year. As August opens, you may get news regarding their spat.

You probably won't like what you hear. Take heart! Beautiful angles among other planets suggest that things are going smoothly, and that harmony is possible in most areas of your life.

Don't let any sudden upsets worry you unduly. There's plenty of time to digest the full implications of whatever arises.

The elements of earth and water are especially blessed, so get outside if possible. Enjoy nature and the outdoors. Connect with the environment, and look beyond mere human affairs. We are, after all, a very small part of life on this planet. Allow Mother Earth herself to strengthen and sustain you.

Such upsets as do occur will most likely centre on your house of friendship, but anything connected with people and places you care about may be affected as well. Don't act in haste. Take some time to mull things over.

If you are sure of what you want to do, the new moon in Leo on Sunday 8 provides an opportunity to act. It's not the best possible moment, though. Hard angles to Saturn and Uranus suggest unforeseen problems, as well as obstacles and delays. You may meet with opposition from an older or more established person, or from the past. But you may also be tempted to take foolhardy risks, or act in ways that you later regret. Be careful. Really think things through. Communicative Mercury near the Sun and Moon offers news, information, and clarity of thought. Make sure you know what you're doing. Seek professional advice if required.

There is another reason why it may be better to wait. At mid-month, Mercury moves into your house of inner needs, which it rules, and connects with energetic Mars in happy angle to Uranus. You may get messages or information that throw new light on the situation. If you've considered all the angles and are sure you wish to act, this is a more favourable moment.

Alternatively, you may come up with new and better ideas at this time. If so, there's still just enough new-moon energy in the air to give you a boost. Act in the days surrounding Monday 16 for best effect.

The next few weeks are likely to be more peaceful than the beginning of the month. Harmony planet Venus, your personal ruler, is moving through your own sun sign, fair-minded Libra. This brings a happy glow to everything you do.

It's an excellent time to pursue your own interests.

On Sunday 22 the Sun moves into Virgo, joining ruling planet Mercury and energetic Mars in your house of inner needs. With so much planetary activity concentrated in this house, you'll feel a major boost in your personal life.

Over the next few weeks, you may begin to find answers and solutions to all sorts of problems. Beautiful angles all over the zodiac wheel shower you with blessings! Past connections may resurface, and mature experience guide you towards sound decisions. There's a balance between old and new, with little in the way of conflict or confrontation. This a wonderful time to press on with existing projects or revisit treasured plans.

Also on Sunday 22 we have a full moon in Aquarius, your house of love. This follows on from the full moon at the end of last month, which was likewise in Aquarius, and brings a far more harmonious atmosphere. Anything you struggled with at the end of July can be brought to a good conclusion now.

Do strive to finish things up in the days surrounding this date. Much of September will be dominated by Mercury's impending retrograde in your own sun sign of Libra, which brings snags and snarlups to everything you do. It really is best to sort things out now if you can.

The next couple of weeks are likely to be peaceful and pleasant, a welcome reward for navigating choppy waters these past few months. Enjoy!

September

The month opens on a joyful note. Happy aspects between most of the planets signal the restoration of understanding and goodwill.

Long-standing issues remain concerning your houses of love, home and family, and shared property and inheritance. These are brought on by the hard angle between stern Saturn in Aquarius and rebellious Uranus (the ruler of Aquarius) in Taurus, which means they won't resolve in a hurry. But they are less inflamed now than before.

With both planets currently retrograde, there's a willing-ness to look back over the past to get at the root of the prob-lem. This is a positive and constructive impulse, so do engage with it in good faith.

Apart from that, things are likely to progress well in most areas of your life. The outlook is especially bright in your house of inner needs, where the Sun and Mars are hosting a party and have invited half the zodiac. You will feel this won-derful energy in everything you do.

On Tuesday 7 a lovely new moon signals a fresh start in this same house of inner needs. It's an excellent time to crack on with existing projects or anything you've had in mind for a while. Uranus and Pluto, both retrograde, beam their best wishes into this house, while nearby Mars provides energetic support. It's a good time to implement well-laid plans.

Act in the days following the new moon, if you can. From mid-month onwards, you may begin to feel the effects of Mercury's impending retrograde. Snags and snarlups will be rife, especially at month's end. Get things sorted out now.

On Tuesday 21 a full moon in Pisces brings something to an end in your house of health and work (which includes all practical steps you take in pursuit of your goals). This could prove to be a fraught time, with aggressive Mars close to the Sun and idealistic Neptune retrograde near the Moon. Will and emotion strive for supremacy. You may come to a painful decision, or experience a distressing revelation. Either way, feelings will run high.

This is not necessarily a bad thing. Reality can be difficult at times, and it's human to respond with both head and heart. Empathy and understanding are key in this situation. Have patience with yourself, and with others.

Powerful Pluto retrograde in lovely angle shows that whatever ends now is for the best. Look to the past for guidance and insight. Allow matters to settle before deciding what to do next.

The very next day, Wednesday 22, the Sun moves into Libra and your birthday month begins. With aggressive Mars nearby, and Mercury about to turn retrograde, you'll experience plenty of static during the next couple of weeks.

A whole lot of issues may bubble up and demand your attention. Take care to deal with them in a methodical manner. Snags, snarlups, delays, and miscommunication will be rife. Make sure everything is crystal clear, with no room for misunderstandings.

Don't be in a hurry to act. A gorgeous new moon in Libra next month will provide a much better opportunity, with generous support from slow-moving planets in your house of love. Give yourself time to gather relevant information and hammer out the details. Early October will provide the perfect moment to implement your plans.

Mercury remains retrograde until mid-October, and the effects will last for a few weeks beyond that, so it may be November before matters are fully resolved. Expect plenty of static during this time. You will feel this more strongly than any other sign, since Mercury rules your house of inner needs (where your aims and plans take shape) and is currently retrograde in your house of self (where your conscious will and action resides).

Look backwards rather than forwards. Take a moment to collect your thoughts. If your plans and preparations are solid, or if you're pursuing existing projects, do nail down the last few details and prepare to launch in mid-October. But if not, consider delaying until a more favourable time.

Other than that, this retrograde isn't likely to be overly troublesome. With so much planetary support, and with all

the outer planets retrograde, you're more likely to find yourself reviewing and revisiting matters from the past. This is
healthy and positive, so have a good clearout and enjoy the
process of settling your affairs.

Progress on most fronts is likely to be slow. Embrace this,
rather than fight against it. Even a sedate pace gets you to the
right destination eventually, and often by a far more scenic
route!

October

This month may be a turning point in many ways. No less than three planets turn direct at mid-month, which creates forward momentum that will last until Christmas. Things won't move fast, but they will get moving again. The tide turns, and blockages crumble away.

You'll feel the effects more strongly than most, since your houses of love and self are affected. Everything that truly matters in your life will start to blossom. It's not a time to leap into action without heeding the consequences, but do put together a workable plan for whatever you want to do, and implement it at mid-month.

Before then, we have a lovely new moon in your own sun sign of Libra on Wednesday 6, which starts the ball rolling. This is an excellent time to act on any plans you made towards the end of last month. Don't expect instant results, but do take decisive and well-considered action, and have faith that the rewards will come in time.

Anything you've been sitting on for a while is also ripe for action. Dust off those dreams!

Pluto in Capricorn, your house of home and family, turns direct on the same day. You may experience a bit of static regarding domestic (or possibly financial) matters around this time. It's nothing serious. Bad news may arrive, as Mercury is retrograde and in hard angle, but happy beams from Venus and Neptune show there is a higher meaning to everything that occurs. Shrug off any setbacks, and look towards the future with confidence.

A few days later, Saturn turns direct. Because Saturn is the ruler of Capricorn, this may connect with whatever's come to light. Watch for any developments in your domestic life. Already you may begin to see the upside to recent events.

A week after that, protective Jupiter and communicative Mercury both turn direct on the same day, Monday 18. With beautiful aspects in support, this could manifest as a happy surprise or other welcome development. Mid-month is likely to be a lovely time, full of positive energy, so do use it for whatever seems right to you.

If you celebrate Christmas or any other holiday towards the end of the year, get your preparations underway. The next two months will be unsettled, with eclipses and hard planetary aspects throwing life into turmoil. Act now if you can, or else leave things be until mid-December.

On Wednesday 20 a full moon in Aries brings something to a close in your house of relationships. With Mars, the ruler of Aries, close to the Sun on the opposite side of the zodiac wheel, and with powerful Pluto in hard angle and still a little groggy from its recent change of direction, you probably won't like what you hear. Some kind of disappointment seems likely, especially in connection with the most important people in your life.

Take heart. Neptune retrograde in happy angle suggests things may not be as bad as they seem. This could be a temporary setback, or it may be that the time just isn't right. If you truly believe this is the right path for you, a new moon in Aries in early April next year provides an excellent chance to try again. Use the intervening time to improve your plans!

Alternatively, you may conclude that whatever ends now just wasn't for you after all. If so, the same new moon will give you a fabulous chance to set off on a different path. Take some time to consider your options.

On Saturday 23 the Sun moves into Scorpio and energises your house of money and personal resources. Nearby Mars adds its own unique brand of vigour, and with lovely angles to protective Jupiter in play, this is a wonderful time to pursue your own interests.

Relationships with other people are especially strong right now, so do reach out if you need assistance or support. It's also an excellent time to take action in joint matters and shared endeavours.

Move fast, though. Grouchy Uranus retrograde in stubborn Taurus, opposite, is engaged in open battle with the mighty Sun. This makes for fireworks!

Radical changes, sudden breakdowns, and unexpected events are on the cards. Situations and relationships that aren't right for you could implode with startling speed. That's not a bad thing, in and of itself. We all need a shakeup from time to time! The real issue is that Mars is on the move, and will confront Uranus directly in the first few days of November.

These two planets don't play nice! Both are aggressive, rebellious, and uncompromising. When they're locked in combat, others are wise to stand well aside. Fierce confrontations, physical injuries, and violent eruptions are possible. Tread with extreme care.

The upshot is that anything you want to get done, especially in financial matters, is best handled right now. Likewise, deal speedily with anything regarding the people you care about the most.

As November approaches, leave well enough alone. Don't risk getting caught in the crossfire.

The Taurus-Scorpio axis will be a battleground for some time yet. In mid-November, a new series of eclipses opens along this axis. The series will bring lasting changes to your houses of money and property (both what you personally own or control, and what you share with others). Whatever you want to do in the realm of financial or material resources, get it done quickly.

Alternatively, sit back and watch the situation unfold. Major changes are afoot, and now is not the time to push through any long-term plans of your own. They could well run aground before properly launched. If you have big ideas, consider putting them on ice until you know how circum-stances shake out.

The series ends in late October 2023, so you have plenty of time in hand. Small stuff can be dealt with now, but save the 'once in a lifetime' moves until the dust has well and truly settled. If your plans are good, they'll keep.

(As always, seek qualified professional advice before making any important financial decisions.)

November

This month will be dominated by a standoff between your houses of money and shared property. A new series of eclipses opens along this axis at mid-month, bringing radical change to your life. The balance between what you personally own or control, and what you share with others (including your cultural heritage and family background) will shift. The lines between what is yours and what is not will be re-drawn.

This can be difficult, but also freeing. You may have less to rely on than you thought, but also less responsibility to bear. Approach the situation with an open mind, and prepare to be flexible. You'll emerge with a lighter cosmic "suitcase" – or perhaps with a more solid sense of support (whether spiritual or material).

You'll feel the tension build well in advance. As the month opens, aggressive Mars and the mighty Sun are both in your house of money and personal resources, while erratic Uranus is retrograde in your house of shared property and inheritance, opposite. This suggests major conflict.

The new moon in Scorpio on Thursday 4 brings these issues into sharp focus. This is a difficult new moon, with stern Saturn in hard angle and aggressive Mars bringing a combative energy to the argument.

With such fierce energies in play, safety is at a premium. Take very great care in all areas of your life. Accidents and injuries are likely. Avoid risk.

Also at this time, you may experience a bit of static in Pisces, your house of health and work. Neptune, the ruler of this sign, turns direct at the beginning of the month after being retrograde since midsummer. Normally we don't much notice the vagaries of this slow-moving planet, but the current upheaval in fellow water sign Scorpio may bring long-standing issues to the fore. Because Neptune is actually travelling through Pisces right now, the effects will be stronger than usual.

Happily, this influence should prove entirely benign. Powerful Pluto sends sympathetic beams from congenial earth sign Capricorn (your house of home and family), while a cluster of forceful planets add their support. Everything you value is blessed by a multitude of beams.

At mid-month, a full moon and lunar eclipse in Taurus brings something to an end in your house of shared property and inheritance. Almost certainly, you won't like the message it brings. Hard angles between planets in Scorpio, Aquarius, and Taurus suggest bad news.

But if you look closer, excellent prospects can be found. Whatever your hopes are, you'll find the means to pursue them. All you need is the right moment. That, sadly, isn't now. Cosmic forces beyond our individual control are revising and re-setting expectations. If things haven't quite worked out for you, this is the time to find out why.

Don't be in a hurry to decide what to do about it. Eclipses bring major shakeups to the area they visit. Once the dust settles, nothing will be quite the same again.

This particular series will continue to overhaul your houses of money and property for the next two years, ending with another lunar eclipse in Taurus at the end of 2023. You have plenty of time to think about what your next step might be.

Just a few days later, on Monday 22, the Sun moves into Sagittarius and shifts the planetary emphasis to your house of everyday routines (including your neighbourhood and workplace). This prepares the ground for the final eclipse in the Gemini-Sagittarius series, which occurs early next month. The series has spent the past eighteen months overhauling your houses of travel, learning, and everyday life, and isn't quite done yet.

Hold fire on anything important, and don't make any major decisions right now, but do keep your antenna up. News and information may arrive in the next few days, as communicative Mercury (the ruler of Gemini) moves into Sagittarius on Wednesday 24. Pay close attention to anything that crops up towards the end of the month.

If you're planning for Christmas or any other holiday around this time of year, hold off on doing anything signific ant. Mid-December will provide lots of opportunity to sort things out. For now, just let the planets have their say.

December

The first half of this month will be all about your house of everyday routines (including your neighbourhood and workplace, and your ordinary environment in general).

In the very first week, on Saturday 4 December, a new moon and solar eclipse in Sagittarius opens a fresh chapter in your day-to-day life. This is the final eclipse in the Gemini-Sagittarius series that started in early June 2020. Then, something ended in this same house of everyday routines. Now, something else is about to begin.

The current eclipse may be confusing at first. Don't let that put you off! Nearby Mercury brings clarity, while wisdom planet Saturn in happy angle offers perspective. Allow things to resolve in their own good time.

There won't be any more eclipses on the Gemini-Sagittarius axis until 2029. You'll have plenty of time to adjust to the changes this series has brought. Right now, the most important thing is to avoid acting in haste. Hold off until you're sure of your information and can see the best path forward. If you must respond to events, do so from a place of calm.

At mid-month, on Monday 14 to be exact, energy planet Mars moves into Sagittarius. This adds extra oomph to your day-to-day life. Lovely angles to Pluto and Venus suggest fabulous developments close to home. You may discover that events under the recent eclipse have set you free.

Pluto and Venus are currently meeting in Capricorn, your house of home and family, and sending happy beams to every planet within their reach. You may have felt the effects as early as mid-November, but now they're taking centre stage. If you have domestic or financial matters to attend to, this is an excellent time to give them your full attention.

Do consider your long-term plans. Pluto is a slow-moving planet, and Venus about to turn retrograde, so patience is a virtue right now. Don't be in a hurry. But with so many beautiful aspects in play, you'll be feeling optimistic about the future. Take your time!

You may experience further complications in the wake of the eclipse. Respond if you feel it's necessary, but don't be in a hurry to initiate anything at all. Allow things to shake out fully before you decide what to do next.

On Sunday 19 harmony planet Venus turns retrograde in congenial Capricorn, your house of home and family. With powerful Pluto in close support, and sympathetic Neptune sending its blessings, this shouldn't prove to be a problem. Rather the opposite, in fact! It's an excellent time to connect with kith and kin.

Also on the same day, a full moon in Gemini brings something to an end in your house of travel and learning. This is a quiet and mostly positive full moon, with Jupiter sending blessings from your house of love. Neptune in hard angle in your house of health and work suggests an element of confusion, so hold off on decisive action. But it's a good time to finish up small matters, including anything that got sidelined by the eclipse earlier this month.

On Tuesday 21 the mighty Sun moves into Capricorn, energising your house of home and family. With harmony planet Venus (your own personal ruler) moving backwards through this sign, and with lots of happy aspects between the planets, this is an excellent time to sort things out before the holidays. Anything that didn't quite get done back in November can be put to bed now without any fuss.

Christmas itself looks splendid, with happy angles all over the chart. Your house of home and family is especially blessed. With so much planetary good cheer around, whatever you do should turn out well!

The long-running battle between Saturn and Uranus may overshadow the festivities, so don't make any big decisions or major commitments (unless you must). Keep things low key. But this energy will mostly be felt on a global scale, far beyond the limits of hearth and home. Stick close to the people you trust and care about. In the end, that's the only thing that matters.

New Year will likewise prove harmonious, at least on the small scale, with lots of happy angles between the planets. Anything connected with the people and places you love is especially blessed. Focus what truly matters in your life, and let the rest of the world sort itself out in its own good time.

A new year is dawning! There is hope for us all.

The Year Ahead: 2022

This year could prove remarkably peaceful, at least by comparison with 2021. Powerful Pluto in grounded Capricorn is deep in conversation with idealistic Neptune in visionary Pisces. This brings hopes, dreams, and wishes to the fore.

Solutions to problems are possible, but not always easy. Hard-nosed Saturn and rebellious Uranus continue their long-standing feud, showing us that revolution must eventually answer to pragmatism.

On the plus side, a cluster of planets in practical Capricorn offer wonderful support to Uranus in fellow earth sign Taurus. Sound reasoning and common sense may yet show the way towards a sustainable future.

The Taurus-Scorpio eclipse series continues, ending in late 2023. This brings profound transformation to your houses of money and property, realigning the balance between what's yours and what you share with others.

There are no other eclipses this year, so consider this a cosmic pause before another great shift of planetary emphasis begins with the Aries-Libra eclipse series next year. This will overhaul your houses of self and relationships, helping you ensure that the most important people in your life are still right for you.

The world is changing. This is good! Listen to your heart, and be guided by your soul.

We are made from stardust. As the planets travel through the heavens, their beams light our path. Where it leads we cannot know. But there is one sure way to find out: by treading it.

***

Goodbye Zoe

Zoe is retiring! This will be the last annual forecast from her at Byrnie Publishing.

Zoe says: "Thank you to my wonderful readers! It's been a joy and a privilege to 'meet' you all. May the stars shine brightly in your lives!"

QUICK GUIDE TO THE HOROSCOPE

A horoscope is a map of the heavens, showing the location of the planets as seen from the Earth. It is divided into twelve sections named after star constellations, known as the signs of the zodiac. The Sun and Moon count as planets, as does Pluto.

The sign in which the Sun was located at the moment of your birth is of huge importance in shaping your fundamental nature and your outlook on life. This is known as your sun sign. Many people who aren't familiar with their full birth horoscope only know their sun sign, so they often refer to it in a shorthand way as their star sign.

In fact, the sun sign only represents one key aspect of your astrological personality: your conscious self. The other eleven signs also represent important areas of lived experience.

All twelve zodiac signs taken together, counting from the sun sign, are known as the solar houses.

By knowing which planets will be in a certain house, and in what angle to other planets in other houses, we can predict the influence they are likely to have in various areas of your life.

Without a detailed individual birth horoscope, as well as knowledge of your personal circumstances, it is not possible for anyone else to predict the exact events you will experience. But you are the expert on your own life! Read the forecasts, and consider how they apply to your specific situation. Then plan accordingly, and be amazed at the results.

SUMMARY OF THE HOUSES

The solar houses are counted from your sun sign forwards through the zodiac wheel. You don't need to know them, because your sun sign governs all that you do, but they can help in understanding why planetary movements "ping" your life in certain areas.

Self: Your own sun sign. This represents your conscious mind, will, and action.

Resources: What you own in the world. Also known as your money house.

Environment: Your ordinary environment. This includes your neighbourhood and workplace.

Home: Your "home base". This includes parents, family of origin, and the property you live in.

Love: What drives your passion. Romance, children, creativity. Anything you do for fun.

Work: How you pursue your goals in life. This connects to your physical health and capabilities, which therefore also fall under this house.

Relationships: Your partnerships with other people, whether personal or professional.

Inheritance: Whatever you draw on but do not control, such as your heritage, shared resources, and anything lent, borrowed, or owed.

Travel: Exploring beyond your ordinary environment. Anything that expands your horizons.

Career: Your public achievements and image. Professional standing. How other people regard you.

Friendship: Your social circle. Wherever you feel you belong in the wider world (outside home, family, or neighbourhood).

Inner needs: Whatever drives your unconscious. Hopes and dreams.

FREQUENTLY ASKED QUESTIONS

Question: I know my Ascendant (Rising Sign) and Moon Sign. Should I read for those as well?

Answer: You can if you want to, but there's no need. The Ascendant or Rising Sign shows your outlook on life and what you tend to manifest naturally. The Moon Sign shows your emotional landscape and how you tend to respond to events. But the Sun Sign shows your sense of self, who you are and what you choose to do. The forecasts are designed to help you plan and execute your own decisions, so the Sun Sign forecast is completely sufficient.

Question: I worry about difficult aspects coming up. Help!

Answer: These can be stressful. Think of them as dammed-up energy. With care, it can be used to good effect. Trust yourself to find a way through. You're stronger than you think!

Question: I can't always time my actions the way you suggest. Is it OK to ignore your advice and do my own thing?

Answer: Absolutely! Always use your own best judgement. You are the expert on your life and circumstances. Do remember that we're all fallible. Astrologers can be wrong, too!

Question: I'd like a detailed individual forecast. Are you taking new clients?

Answer: Unfortunately, no.

ABOUT THE AUTHOR

Zoe Buckden has been an astrologer in private practice for over thirty years. She lives in the north of England with several cats and the occasional hedgehog.

ABOUT BYRNIE PUBLISHING

We are a small independent publisher specialising in genre fiction and popular nonfiction.